CIR'CUM·NAV'I·GA'TION

Cyn. Zarco

Tooth of Time
Books
1986

Copyright © 1986, Cyn.Zarco
Copyright © 1986, cover photo, Vincent Hughes Frye

Some of these poems appeared in:

Jambalaya: An Anthology of Four Poets, Yardbird Lives!, Yardbird Reader II, III, V, Breaking Silence, Califia, Bridge, Time to Greez!!, Quilt I, Liwanag, Essence, Contact II, Zone Magazine and *California Living.*

Cover design: Sue Wilder & Cyn.Zarco
ISBN 0-940510-13-8

Then the captain said that if they became Christians he would leave them weapons which Christians use, and that his king had ordered him to do this. And he showed them that they could not have intercourse with their women without great sin, because they were heathen. And he assured them that since they were Christians, the devil would no longer appear to them except at the point and extremity of death.
   —from *Magellan's Voyage*,
      the journal of Antonio Pigafetta,
      April 9, 1521
      Cebu, Philippines

TABLE OF CONTENTS

WHAT THE ROOSTER DOES BEFORE MOUNTING
What the Rooster Does Before Mounting / 11
Once Upon a Seesaw With Charlie Chan / 12
Pacific Lover / 14
Flipochinos / 15
Asparagus / 16
What Emiliano Said to Me One Day at Pescadero Beach / 17
lolo / 18
Chinese Checkers / 19
o / 20
Cultural Exchange / 21
4¼% Interest / 22
Emergency Poem 1973 / 23
Still Life / 24
Poem in Nueva York / 25
Orleans Hotel, NYC, 1980 / 26

THE MUSE CONSIDERED AS A WAYWARD HUSBAND
The Muse Considered as a Wayward Husband / 29
Sitcom for a Ghost Writer / 30
Irony / 31
Teaching Poetry / 32
An Altitude for Angels / 33
New Descending A Staircase / 34
Duet / 35

NIGHTS
Nights / 39
(V-poem) / 40
The Fountain of Youth / 41
Rerun / 42
Saxophonetyx / 43
Lyrix for Rodolfo / 44
Manila Bay / 46
Bad Timing / 48
Magdalena's Vision / 49
Vanishing Act / 50

POP FLY
In Memory of Forgetting / 53
A I R / 54
Zelda & the Safecracker / 56
The Night the Clocks Turned Back / 58
Cocktails / 59
Pop Fly / 60
Boomerang / 62
Portrait of an Artist as a Young Ball / 63

.WHAT THE ROOSTER DOES BEFORE MOUNTING.

What the Rooster Does Before Mounting

Gustavo said,
"Your poems are like samba,
some even tango on the page
as if part of some strange ritual—
what the rooster does before mounting."

Gustavo said,
"In Argentina, I was in love
with Che. Even my father,
the old prick, gave him money."

Then, said Gustavo,
"You did not choose me; I chose you,"
and made me sit down while he took over
my kitchen.

I sat in a yellow chair
and watched him chop vegetables—

    carrots   bell pepper   onions

Once Upon a Seesaw With Charlie Chan

i think i was three
beneath the guava tree
next to the doghouse in the front yard
with the crisscross bamboo fence
the seesaw was pastel
pink green and yellow and i
a nutbrown child with black hair
i had the up-and-down-of-it down pat
as i straddled the wooden plank with chubby knees
facing a boy nicknamed charlie chan
it was a slow afternoon
wives winning at mah-jongg
maids eavesdropping
i may have been daydreaming
of the other playground
the one with the swings and silver seesaws
the one that survived the tornado
or maybe my mind lingered
on the fingering of a piano
a blue dragonfly whizzing nearby
i soared above it all
above the red hibiscus flowers
and the sweet banana tree
above the bougainvillea and the gardenia
charlie had beads for eyes
that was how he got his name
he was smaller than i
and i was the girl

i don't know what got into him
as evenly weighted we swung side-to-side
he jumped on his seat like satan
up smack between my legs
a wooden whack drew blood
i searched for the trickle's source
no wound or cut
no sign of origin
charlie ran home
i ran to mother
she swabbed me with alcohol and muttered
no explanation
the bleeding stopped
there was no pain
and i never seesawed with charlie chan again

Pacific Lover

naked i write
coming back from the city
coming back from the intestines
of san francisco
thinking of my mother on the freeway
thinking how we must learn
to automobile
to stickshift
to find a parking space
in the heart of america
(turn your wheels to the curb
so your car won't run away)
runaway in the middle of the night
while we sleep
barefoot
she in her negligee
and i in my skin
our souls in manila
in leyte in balara
we sleep and dream
of different continents
she hears the atlantic
my father snoring
the waves of the pacific
is a tongue in my ear
i dream
of death
please bury my body
under a mango tree
feed the fruit
to my friends

Flipochinos

when a brown person
gets together
with a yellow person
it is something like
the mating of a chico and a banana
the brown meat of the chico
plus the yellow skin of the banana
take the seed of the chico for eyes
peel the banana for sex appeal
lick the juice from your fingers
and watch your step

Asparagus

There's a washcloth
with a picture of asparagus
in my bathroom.

Did you know
that Pilipinos were picked
to grow asparagus in the West
because they were short
and built closer to the ground?

I'm 5'3". I don't use
that washcloth anymore.

What Emiliano Said to Me One Day at Pescadero Beach

This beach
has changed
since I've
been here,

he said,
digging
for clams
that weren't there
anymore. And,

What do you see
in that cloud
over there?
I see
a cloud
with long hair
face the sun;
I see
my friends.

You roll
up your pants
like a real
Pilipino.

I can't walk down the beach
with shoes on. And,
my hands, I just want
to keep my hands
warm....

Here, put them
on my belly
where I am
warmest.

lolo died yesterday.
    they called him bill
    short for villamor
    i called him lolo
    lolo doming
    grandfather
    even though he was my mother's uncle
    even though he wasn't my real
    grandfather
    i called him lolo
    star barber at the star barber shoppe
    on 6th & mission
    he talked about the navy
    the american navy
    he showed me the calligraphy
    on his silver lighter
    he showed me his diploma
    from cosmetology school
    lolo
    lolo doming
    hung out with the boys
    at the mabuhay gardens
    gambled in reno
    got drunk with the pinoys
    kumpadres mga kasamahan
    died dancing
    on treasure island

Chinese Checkers

Life
is a game
of Chinese checkers.

The opposition
is another color

& no one is Chinese.

o
san francisco slow and cold
i have taken up smoking
and drinking
jamaican rum & coffee
walk reggae
in multicolored ragamuffin chinese brocade
down streets of uptight korean landlords
in my straw borsalino at night
white shades drawn
in the daytime
eyes peeking out of peking
at paradise
across the street
we meet
eyes cross
lips thin
to full brown
blowing songs
of alto & soprano saxophone
palm trees
they surreptitiously nod
to no one in particular
building railroads
crossties
to nowhere

Cultural Exchange

There's a ballerina next door
who wears kimonos and reads Shakespeare
in bed.

Some nights
she comes to visit me.

Tonight we traded a bookshelf
for a full-length mirror.

4¼% Interest

I cannot squeeze love
out of you.

You are like
the Bank of America.

There has been
a $230 error in your favor.

Emergency Poem 1973
—for Nicanor Parra

Today's American car
is like a woman who won't
start until she fastens
her seat belt.
She screams
when you leave the key
in the ignition
long after the ride
has ended.

Still Life

3 widows
in an antique house
dusting

Poem in Nueva York

phantasmagorillaorgasmiasmacharismamama
diaphragmdiarrheacatarrhcatatoniccatastrophicmascara
maracascaracasbarakastrakatakas
attack us
attack us
attack us
atticalunatica
bakitkanapakaloka
guayabano y banana mo
mi alma y tu almo
en mi poema
sorpresa

Orleans Hotel, NYC, 1980

each day
another
chip of paint
falls from
my ceiling

i never know
when one
will fall

it is slow
chinese
water torture

it can make
you crazy
like the snow
in winter

you look up
always waiting
for the next one

.THE MUSE CONSIDERED AS A WAYWARD HUSBAND.

The Muse Considered as a Wayward Husband

This love affair's been going on
for almost sixteen years now. At first
he used to surprise me. Now I sit
and wait for him. You'd think
he'd be more consistent what with
all this carrying on, but no,
he's just as fickle as ever,
comes and goes as he pleases, stays
awhile then I may not see him again
for weeks. I always take him back though.
I guess he knows I still love him.
I've got no choice.
There's nothing else like him.

Sitcom for a Ghost Writer

My genius can't sleep.
My laundry goes unwashed.
I need new costumes, new shoes.
I need a haircut.
I want to write but I can't.
I fear success but want it badly.
I can't stand him, but I love him madly.
I'm losing control.
I'm losing my mind.
There is no tranquilizer, no cure, no silence.
(I can't find it.)
The song goes unwritten.
The poem unrealized.
The groceries are invisible;
only fog fills my refrigerator.
I start to eat it
and my vision gets cloudy.
Even the cigarettes I smoke
contribute to the smog of my existence.
My dreams are disappearing.
The role I've written for myself
is getting cut out of the play.
God calls me
but I'm never home these days.

Irony

My typewriter is warm.
A poet called me
on the phone and said,
"I can't stand you. I have
to get high now."
Then she
hung
up.

Teaching Poetry
—for Mark Strand

You walk into a room of voices.
You are wearing a pink sweater.

It is snowing and a woman walks across the lawn.
She is naked and she does not see you.

You want her but the voices keep you from jumping
    out the window.
They are reciting poetry.

The woman outside is headless.
She motions to you.

You pull off your sweater.
Another pink sweater appears.

You peel off the pink sweater.
There is always another pink sweater.

You unscrew your head.
You feel much better now.

An Altitude for Angels

The view from the plane is modern:
babies' breath against a pale blue cloth,
the smooth spooning of waves,
the undefined line of the horizon.

All it takes is one brushstroke
to cast a soft rose haze
in subtle tones of the Japanese.

The sunlight cleans the air.

This must be the altitude for angels—
why men envy them.

New Descending a Staircase

new
eyes new
face new body
new hands new fingers
new whiskers new voice new
neck new eyes new ears new nose
newness new thighs new penis new balls
new kiss new tongue new teeth new lips new
arms new shoulders new chest new armpit smell
new hair new nipples new breasts new breath new
thigh muscles sigh new rear end yes new cock getting
newer o new knees new ankles new toes new feet new sheet

Duet

Music takes shape in many forms
Sometimes the light is dim
the door ajar
A man may be sleeping on the floor
She walks into his shadow
There is a mirror
To her it means so much more
than two figures exchanging sound
She wants him to touch that part
It's hard to
She peels the skin

.NIGHTS.

"Sexual intercourse is the human counterpart of the cosmic process."
—ancient Chinese proverb

Nights

When I'm without you
I sleep on the couch
or in my bed with books,
pen & paper.

I can't decide
which I love best—
you lying next to me
like an open book
or an open book
lying next to me.

(V-poem)

He sat
on the bed
to put his socks on
but first
kissing
my bare shoulder.
"There is an angel in me
that I am constantly shocking."
That is a line from one of Ferlinghetti's poems.
At the beginning of his ass is a neat
V
like an arrow pointing
out the best features of his body.
I lay in bed and think of that.
That'll keep me going
for days.

The Fountain of Youth

"Love is never equal,"
a 38-year-old man discovered.

He followed her to Florida,
just like Ponce de León.

Rerun

"I don't like it
when you comb your hair back like that."

When a lover returns
from the past, it is like
seeing a movie for the second time.

Since you already know the ending
you don't have to pay attention
to the plot.

Saxophonetyx

I've heard all about musicians
They take love, don't give love
'cause they're savin it for the music

Got to be so one night I was watching him
take a solo, and when he closed his eyes
everyone in the club closed their eyes
The first thing I saw was my shoes
float out of his horn
my favorite leopard-skin high-heel shoes
the left foot, then the right one
followed by my black silk stockings
with the seam down the back
my best hat and all that
were floating in the air like half notes
like they belonged to no one
least of all to me

I tried to close my eyes
but I couldn't
Out flew my blue silk scarf
my alarm clock
my alligator suitcase
even last month's phone bill

He kept on playing that horn
as if nothing even happened
and when I slowly closed my eyes
I saw his fingers wrap around my waist
my spine turn into saxophone keys
my mouth become his mouthpiece
and there was nothing left in the room
but mercy

Lyrix for Rodolfo

o
bein your woman
is a 24-hour/allnightstand/jukeboxmovie
i'm auditionin for leading lady
but
everybody's tryin to get into the act

i don't wanna be second fiddle
i wanna be lead guitar
i don't wanna be the costar
i wanna be the star

o bein your woman
is a pain-in-the-ass/sweet-thingin lulu
you got my juju
i got the do-nuthin do-nuthin doodoo

i don't wanna be second fiddle
i wanna be lead guitar
i don't wanna be no costar
i wanna be your star

from egypt to asia
i longed for you
miami drove me crazy
i horned for you

will you be my baby
will you be my man
i need you in my china
forget about japan

this second best
don't pass the test
this is me talkin
the best in the west

so
will you be my baby
will you be my man
i need you in my china
forget about japan

Manila Bay

love is never so real as real life
when the rent's due
& you don't even know
what day it is

i took the bus downtown
cause i was locked out of my house
my lover in bed on a sunny day
i took the bus downtown
& found you on the shelf

you were a sailor
ready to sail into my harbor
i am the ocean
i said
manila bay

o
love is never so real as real life
when your best boyfriend
becomes your best friend's boyfriend
& you don't even know
what your name is

you got to
keep your secrets quiet
you never know
what
you never know
the words flow on & on

i am on the road
you say
we are all travelers
i say

you got to
keep all doors open
to let the wind blow
in & out
you got to
keep all doors open
to let the love go
in & out

there is only time here
there is only sound here

dance for me
lights out

Bad Timing

it was your pink
feet
& your water eyes
& the way you sang
about green apples
in the shower
we made love
many times
but soon i found myself
sleeping away from you
my shiny black hair
tickled your nose
your rough beard
scratched my face
we never ate onions together
it was always time
to go to the bathroom
when you got hot
i needed the sleep
when i got hot
you were watching
kelly's heroes
in your boxer shorts
i soon began to sneeze
it was your pink
feet
& your water eyes
my toes
got colder
faster

Magdalena's Vision

I
loosed
the knot
of cloth
around
his waist
and knelt
at his
feet.
"Father, forgive her for she knows."
I cupped the staff of life and bathed
it lovingly with my cat's tongue. He
rolled his eyes toward Heaven. The
white
cloth
dropped
to the
ground.
He filled
my mouth
and drops
of blood
& sweat
fell
from
his
brow.
I
plucked
the crown
of thorns
from
his head
and wiped
his forehead,
then kissed
his face, the
bowl of
his shoulder,
his breasts,
his thighs . . . .

The skies parted. I freed his feet and hands and sealed his wounds.

Vanishing Act

    i.   time passses
           empty spaces
           love lost

   ii.   time passes
           empty spaces

  iii.   time passes

  iv.

.POP FLY.

In Memory of Forgetting

She closed her eyes when she made love, that was how she escaped the longing, the embrace when he was gone. To her it was the man lapping between her legs, the strong stroke of loving, the kiss. She closed her eyes and did not suck in his tongue. This she might remember—the sight of him slipping into her, the look on his face, his heart opening in the small shape of his mouth. She closed her eyes and started to forget, forgetting as soon as he touched her that he touched her there and that way. She did not want to remember how he felt inside her as she moved to his slow motion, to his time. She covered her eyes with a raised arm to stop the light that edged its way around his waist, the firm curve of his backside, the length of his thigh. She saw nothing. Even when she gave him her cry her eyelids stayed shut.

A I R

It wasn't that he loved her. No, that wasn't it at all. He was fascinated by her—the way she walked into the room, her offstage manner, the faint gold chain she wore around her ankle. He had never seen a woman like her. He just wanted to find out who she was, smiling under that broad-brimmed summer hat she wore with MEXICO embroidered in bold red letters across the top like she had been there in the Twenties when things were hot. She was hot. Her brown skin wet as she stepped out of an antique porcelain bathtub with only that far-off look like Aphrodite out of a conch shell but with black hair flowing.

No, it wasn't that he loved her. That much she knew. Not that she didn't pretend that sometimes she saw love there in his eyes, dark and oval like the seeds of the sweet brown chico fruit she used to eat as a child. Something stirred there, but it was only his heartbeat she heard after making love, the rapid fanfare of a snare drum announcing someone new approaching.

When he had been with her a week or so, long enough to tell if something was going to happen, she asked him if they were falling in love now, asked him in that soft cello voice of hers across the table in a Japanese restaurant between bites of pink sushi and thin sake as she twirled a paper parasol counterclockwise.

He wasn't the kind of man who fell in love or longed to tell of it, but one who loved them all, loved to watch the unraveling of it, loved them like kites on long string when there was wind.

And there wasn't even a breeze that night. And it was hot as the clock ran and she wondered what he was up to this time when she felt like loving him.

And it wasn't that she loved him. At least, not yet, because she was the goldfish in this love story and the goldfish bowl was on top of the television where the late afternoon light hit it crisp as a cymbal would shoot prisms it if were sound.

And the only sound in the room was the sound of hand-clapping, clapping against an echo she remembered once in a dream. Or was it a telephone ringing in Chinatown, a love letter on the pavement, or her mother's voice telling her that when love comes, run from it. Run fast. If he loves you, he'll run after you. If he doesn't, you're gone.

Zelda & the Safecracker

Because he did not send for her she did not leave the room. Mail dropped through a slot in the door. Groceries were phoned in. The laundry was delivered, freshly washed and folded, wrapped in blue paper tied crisscross with white string. Zelda thought of nothing else. First, his eyes searing into her being. Second, his fingertips reaching out to her in the dark, wanting her with the desperation of a blind man searching for the surface of an object.

It took her by surprise. The passion in his hands, the force of his desire coursing through him, through her. He was foreign to her, blond, so unlike her physical body one would never take them for lovers. But it wasn't enough for Zelda to discover his body and thank god for it. It wasn't enough for her to feel his flesh against her cheek. She loved him, loved him with the heart he so effortlessly opened like a safecracker tumbling a lock even an expert locksmith could not break open.

Zelda was the older one and the woman. Though he cherished her kisses and guided them, she doubted whether he suspected what fate had arranged. Her desire for him frightened her. Knowing that one man had made a bull's-eye of her heart stripped her naked, yet the joy of finding a man capable of such an act gave her a new sense of hope.

They were standing in a public place, a place unsuited for raw displays of emotion, a place devoid of tears. Zelda wanted to tell him she loved him. Nothing else made any sense. But she was afraid. She couldn't bear to hear him explain the logic of their lives in everyday terms.

He kissed both cheeks. She let him go to the other side of the equator where their worlds would be upside down. From below the pit of her stomach rose an ache that could only be the woman inside her begging for the man, clutching for him.

The Night the Clocks Turned Back

She couldn't wait and neither could he after that first spring breeze blew her blouse off one shoulder. He said she made the first move and she said he did, but after chimichangas and margaritas at El Bandito's, she would have followed him anywhere.

She liked the way he walked, liked that slow, easy gait of his, as if he had some place to go and all the time to get there. She didn't know where he was going, he only wanted to walk in the cool night air, yet she felt his body gravitate toward her place.

They stopped in Washington Square. Two teenagers stood locked in a fierce embrace. The cops chased the big kids out of the playground. He found a bench to sit on. She put her head in his lap, and when he bent down to kiss her she felt the wind at her back blowing through the wooden slats.

"We better take this some place private," was all he said.

He was easy. He gave himself to her with no reservations. He slid into her bed with the grace of a cat coming home.

She didn't ask for more. She didn't get more. And, when she asked for more, he answered that he never asked for more.

"I don't want anymore," he said, lighting a joint.

Cocktails

*"An event in the present can influence
and/or cause an event in the future."*

—from "Three Diamonds,"
Gerard Malanga

He was wearing a pink T-shirt, ballerina pink, with a bright green alligator gaping over his left tit. She was wearing a low-cut V-neck sweater, black like her hair and the space cut around them, black as the shiny baby grand sitting at the edge of the room.

It was cocktails at Gracie Mansion. He was staring into the crowd as if he had something to look at. She gazed into his leather bag. He slung it low and open. There were a few good cameras in there. She looked up at his face. His eyes sat in his skull. Some kind of Siamese-cat blue.

"It was San Francisco, over ten years ago," she said. "You had a bottle of wine in one hand and an Italian in the other." Had they both been naked he would have grazed her with his cock when the half-filled silver tray of hors d'oeuvres pushed him closer to her.

Pop Fly

"Got any drugs?"

They were watching the World Series on TV. The Dodgers were leading the Yankees, three to one, man on first. She couldn't keep her mind on the game.

"No," she said, absentmindedly. "No drugs at all. Just this here." She pointed to the space between her legs. She didn't know why she said that. It just flew out of her mouth, the way a pop fly off a baseball bat lands in a catcher's mitt. She was thinking about his legs; his thighs looked thicker since she saw him last. She looked around the room. Tuesday must be maid day. No dirty dishes in the kitchen; no toothpaste dribble in the sink.

He squeezed her gams. He must have read her mind. "Still got those big legs," he said as they went to a commercial. She flexed then pointed her toes. "Must be the life downtown," was her answer. "All that walking around . . ." She started to think of last summer, of the baseball games in Central Park, the Sunday she stopped to watch Cafe Central win the pennant, all because the shortstop had this way of hunching over and wriggling his ass.

"Want another glass of wine?" He was halfway into the kitchen during a dog food commercial.

"All right."

Had they been madly in love or just hot for each other, they would have lost all sense of time by now. A sub was called in to pitch in the bottom half of the ninth inning. The pitcher cursed his way back to the dugout.

"See that little guy?" he said, pointing to the screen. "That guy makes a million dollars a year."

"That kid?" She sat up.

"Yeah . . . one million dollars."

"He can't be over eighteen . . . ."

She could hear him brush his teeth in the bathroom as she undressed herself in the dark.

Boomerang

"If you want a man to fall in love with you," said George, leaning so close to the hot puff of paratha bread that it formed a halo around his head, "don't fuck him on the first date."

"Why not?" said Mattie, waiting to hear his answer.

"Because," he whispered, as if he were about to let out a secret, "all men are dogs." They both laughed so hard the couple sitting behind them turned to stare. "Seriously," George continued, "if a woman gives it up on the spot, the game's over. But if she just holds out until he asks her again, she might have a chance."

The waiter arrived with a plastic tray full of small dishes of dahl, chutney, curry, and saffron rice. "But," said Mattie, "what if the *man* gives it up on the first date?" That's what George liked about Mattie. She was always one step ahead of him. "Like I said—dogs," he repeated.

George mopped up the last of the concoction of curry sauce, dahl, and red onions swimming on his plate. "I *love* Indian food," he slurred. "I could eat here everyday." Mattie poked at the remains of a chicken leg boomeranged on her plate. "I thought the way to a man's heart was through his stomach."

"Not when you can eat like this for under five dollars," George said, wiping his mouth clean with a mustard-colored napkin.

Portrait of an Artist as a Young Ball

His good side calls me on the phone. It's one o'clock and he just got back from a party. Two parties. He's bored, he says. If I wasn't asleep he'd take me out for a drink. He's being polite, sweet even. I could torture him now, drive a stake through his heart for the time he broke mine. But I say yes, I'll meet him in 15 minutes, because I want to see the guy, even though I know the guy won't talk. I jump into the shower, throw on a black knit sweater, black jacket, tangerine pants, and white sneakers.

I walk over to his place. I ring the bell. He opens the door and grins. I say hello, then walk past him to look at two unfinished floating-penguin paintings in black, red, and white. I like them. They make me laugh. He notices my red Mao button and says he's got one like it. I take a good, long look at him in this big navy coat with stripes. He looks great, even though most people would think otherwise, not knowing Comme des Garcons.

I ask him for a glass of water. He walks me over to the kitchen, then stands there like I should know where the glasses are.

"I could use a glass," I say. He opens the dishwasher and hands me an empty glass instead of filling it with water first. He runs upstairs. When he asks me where I feel like going, I can't think of the right setting for the two of us.

"Let's just go outside," I say.

He has to buy cigarettes. As we walk by a high-rise construction site I steer him across the street. He understands paranoia. I mention a few places I don't feel like going to right then—Great Jones, La Gamelle, Odeon—and he says nothing fancy, which is alright with me because I don't feel like too many white people around. I say, "This was your idea. Where do you go?" The only thing he comes up with is the Ritz Carlton. He says they have HBO there. My eyes get big. I like HBO. I don't care for the Ritz too much, but I like to watch video. "They have HBO at the bar at the Ritz?" He tells me that he has an apartment there, so I say okay, not thinking it could be a hotel room.

We get in a cab. I ask him for a smoke. He lights a Gauloises. I lean back for the ride. The cabbie makes a U-turn at Central Park South to the front door of the Ritz. No one's around but the doorman. When the door opens to his apartment, it's a hotel room alright, with a king-size bed in the middle and ivory sheets turned down. There are three Godiva chocolates wrapped in gold foil on each bedside table. He turns on HBO then walks over to the phone to order room service. "What do you want?" he asks me. Jack Nicholson answers: "I'd like a chicken salad sandwich. Hold the lettuce and tomato...." It's the diner scene from *Five Easy Pieces*.

He sits down at a desk facing Central Park, in an antique chair that's more like a throne, and there's nowhere for me to sit except for the bed, which is directly behind him, or the floor. I settle on the floor, but it makes me feel as if I'm one of his royal subjects, so I get up and walk around the room. He rolls a joint. I find a bottle of Perrier in a silver champagne bucket. There's a knock at the door. An attractive blonde wearing a tuxedo walks in balancing a silver tray.

"Look! A girl penguin!" I say, delighted. The door closes.

He brings me a Remy. He ordered me two. I drink it fast. I'm nervous but I want to be cool. I try talking.

"Do you work in periods?" I ask, then explain that some artists do their best work in the wintertime.

"I paint everyday," he says, lighting a joint the size of a cigar. "When I'm not painting, I do backgrounds." I walk around the room some more, but this time I'm looking for a can opener.

"I like to do drugs, paint, eat . . . and some other things." He says that. I say, "I like to do some other things . . . ."

He's biting his fingernails. I move his hand from his mouth and touch his fingertips. He doesn't move. I don't know what to do now. I want to look at his hands. I love men's hands. He won't open his hand. His hands are like the hands of an old black man. Veins pop like roots, and there's a dark mole in the middle of his right hand. It is like the mole on my right hand, only mine is brown.

"Moles have special meaning," I tell him. "A mole on the hand means you have talent. It also means that a lot of money passes through your hands." I move closer to him and whisper, "I have a mole on my heart."

He shoots me a long look like he's reaching out to me with his eyes but his body's paralyzed. I walk behind him to caress his forehead. I am caressing his mind. It is heavy, full of thought. I loosen his collar. I smooth his shoulders, feel the taut upper muscles of his arms, run my hand across his heart. He snatches it and brings it down to feel his cock, big and hard, under his trousers. As he unbuttons his fly, I unbutton his white shirt. He takes my hand and wraps it around his cock. I walk slowly around the chair to sit between his legs. I stroke his cock like I'm stoking a fire. I kiss it once, twice. I look into his face. I unbutton the last two buttons on his shirt. He wants my mouth. I open his shirt as if it were a book and find a long scar on his belly.

"What happened?" I ask, my right hand still paying attention.
"I was hit by a car," he answers.
"Was it a Buick?" I say, prolonging the seduction.
"It was white."

I pull my sweater up above my left tit to show him my scar, a semicircle around the nipple. He squeezes my right breast then reaches down to feel my ass. I show him another scar on my bottom lip, then I kiss his mouth. I suck his cock good. I lift up my sweater to show him the drawstring at my waist. He pulls it free, then jumps out of his seat to throw my body on the bed. He pulls off his pants. I pull off my pants and the black sweater falls to the floor. As I lie down on the bed he straddles my chest and aims his cock into my mouth. My mouth opens. Before I get a chance to say anything, he hops off and flips me on my stomach to enter me from behind. It is too easy. I squirm to face my woman half to his man. I'm pinned down like a wrestler on the mat. I don't like it. It's too impersonal. I want to hold him tight, wrap my legs around him, rock him hard. He lies still. It is over, but his cock stays warm in my womb. I want to say "Don't fuck me," so I roll him over on his stomach and sit on his spine. I press my mouth to his ear.

"You cheat," I whisper. "You're a spoiled brat."

He stares at me out of the corner of one eye and says, "I spoil myself."

Cyn. Zarco was born in Manila and moved to Miami at the age of 9. She studied journalism at the University of California in Berkeley and has an M.F.A. in writing from Columbia University. Co-author of *Wild Style*, a Simon & Schuster book, she was first published in 1973 by Ishmael Reed in *Yardbird Reader*. She now lives in New York and is writing a novel.

An edition of 750 copies set in 10 point
Sabon using Warren's Antique Book Paper,
printed by West Coast Print
Center & published by
Tooth of Time Books
634 E. Garcia,
Santa Fe
New Mexico
87501

Thanks to the
National Endowment for the Arts
for their support for this publication.

Tooth
of Time
Books may be
ordered direct from
the following distributors:
Book People: 2929 Fifth St., Berkeley, Ca. 94710
Inland Book Co.: P.O. Box 261 East Haven, Ct. 06512
Bookslinger: 330 E. Ninth, Saint Paul, Mn. 55101
S.P.D.: 1784 Shattuck Ave., Berkeley, Ca. 94709